D1613726

Reading American History

The Declaration of Independence

Written by Melinda Lilly
Illustrated by Marty Jones

Educational Consultants

Kimberly Weiner, Ed.D
Betty Carter, Ed.D

Rourke
Publishing LLC
Vero Beach, Florida 32963

www.rourkepublishing.com

**For Michee, Jeremie, Dorcelle and Grace Lotemo, recent citizens of the United
States.
—M. J.**

Designer: Elizabeth J. Bender

Library of Congress Cataloging-in-Publication Data

Lilly, Melinda.
    The Declaration of Independence / Melinda Lilly, illustrated by Marty Jones.
       p. cm. -- (Reading American history)
    Summary: A simple introduction to Independence Day and the writing of the
Declaration of Independence.
    ISBN 1-58952-359-8
    1. Fourth of July--Juvenile literature. 2. United States. Declaration of
Independence--Juvenile literature. [1. Fourth of July 2. Holidays 3. United States.
Declaration of Independence.] I. Jones, illus. II. Title.

E286 .A1393 2002
394.2634--dc21
                                    2002017844

Cover Illustration: Thomas Jefferson stands in front of Independence
Hall with the Declaration of Independence.

Printed in the USA

Time Line

Help students follow this story by introducing important events in the Time Line.

1774   First Continental Congress meets.

1775   The Battle of Concord and Lexington

1776   Thomas Jefferson writes the Declaration of Independence.

1776   The Continental Congress adopts the Declaration of Independence.

1783   Revolutionary War ends.

1797   John Adams becomes the second president of the United States.

1801   Thomas Jefferson becomes the third president of the United States.

The year is 1776.

England rules **America**.

English **soldiers** in America

Many in America want to be free of England.

Men who want to be American soldiers

8

John Adams asks **Thomas Jefferson** to write the **Declaration of Independence.**
It will tell why Americans want to be free.

Thomas Jefferson and John Adams

"I will do as well as I can,"
says Jefferson.

Thomas Jefferson

Jefferson writes for 18 days.

In Jefferson's room

Jefferson takes the Declaration of Independence to the **Continental Congress.**

Jefferson goes to Independence Hall.

The Congress votes on the
Declaration of Independence.

The vote

The vote is yes!

Now all will know why America must be free.

Yes!

It is July 4, 1776—**Independence Day**!

After the vote

Word List

Adams, John (AD emz, JON)—Second president of the United States

America (uh MER ih kuh)—The land that became the United States

Continental Congress (kon ten EN tul KON gress)—A legislative group that met in America during and after the Revolutionary War

Declaration of Independence (dek leh RAY shun OV in dih PEN dens)—The document by which the Continental Congress declared the American colonies to be free of England.

England (ING glund)—Part of the country of Great Britain and the United Kingdom

Independence Day (in dih PEN dens DAY)—July 4, 1776, the day that the Continental Congress adopted the Declaration of Independence

Jefferson, Thomas (JEF er sen, TOM us)—The third president of the United States, Thomas Jefferson wrote the Declaration of Independence.

soldiers (SOLE jerz)—People who serve in the military

Books to Read

Barrett, Marvin. *Meet Thomas Jefferson*. Random House, 2001.

Freedman, Russell. *Give Me Liberty: The Story of the Declaration of Independence.* Holiday House, 2001.

Jones, Veda Boyd. *Thomas Jefferson: Author of the Declaration of Independence*. Chelsea House, 2000.

Walker, Jane C. *John Adams*. Enslow Publishers, 2002.

Websites to Visit

www.loc.gov/exhibits/jefferson/

www.nara.gov/exhall/charters/declaration/decmain.html

www.nara.gov/exhall/charters/declaration/dechist.html

http://memory.loc.gov/const/abt_declar.html

www.ibiscom.com/jefferson.htm

Index